C000173110

THE WISDOM

of the

CHRISTIAN
MYSTICS

TIMOTHY FREKE

 A GODSFIELD BOOK

First published in Great Britain in 1999
by Godsfield Press Ltd, a division of
David and Charles Ltd, Laurel House, Station Approach
Alresford, Hants, SO24 9JH, U.K.

10 9 8 7 6 5 4 3 2 1

Designed by the
Bridgewater Book Company

Printed and bound in Hong Kong

ISBN 1-899434-97-6

CONTENTS

Introduction

Mysticism is the spiritual essence of Christianity. The great Christian mystics, however, have often found themselves horribly persecuted as heretics by the established Churches for their outrageous claims and idiosyncratic ways. The mystics are not content to have a relationship with God via priests and institutions, but look inside themselves to know God directly. When they do, God is revealed as an all–embracing love that unites the universe into one indivisible whole. In communion with God, the mystics no longer experience themselves as separate individuals but as expressions of the Oneness. God is the only reality. God is everything. God does everything. This mystical vision is not a psychological anomaly; it is the natural state. Human beings fail to experience it only because they believe themselves to be separate from God, when in fact He is their very essence. All mystical practices are designed to dispel this pernicious illusion of separateness.

The teachings that the mystics have left for us are not their opinions about God for us to believe or disbelieve. They are testimonies to the possibility of certain intuitive knowledge of

the Truth, that may tempt us with their sublime intensity to make the mystical journey for ourselves. The 16th-century Spanish mystic, St. John of the Cross, writes, "God does not reserve the high vocation of mystical contemplation for certain souls only. On the contrary he wants all to embrace it, but finds few who will permit Him to work such exalted things for them." The very purpose of human life is to come to knowledge of God, and if we simply turn toward God we will find that He has been waiting for us all along. The 17th-century French mystic, Brother Lawrence, assures us "Knock, persevere in knocking, and I guarantee that He will answer."

I The God of the Mystics

The sublime God of the mystics is more than a particular divine being with characteristics and a personality. God is the Oneness that unites everything. "All things are interdependent," says the 14th-century German mystic Meister Eckhart, for whom God is the unifying "Being of all beings." From the greatest to the most insignificant, God is the existence of all that is, and also the nothing from which all things arise. He is both visibly manifest in the abundance of the sensual world, and invisibly present in the hidden emptiness of the soul that experiences it.

> " In the reality, intuitively known by the mystics,
> we can no longer speak of Father, Son, and Holy
> Spirit, nor of any creature, but only One Being, that
> is the super-essence of all. "
>
> RUYSBROEK

“ If I were to say "God exists," this would not be true.
He is being beyond being. He is a nothingness
beyond being. This is why St. Augustine says "The
best thing to be said about God is silence."

You must love God as not-God, not-Spirit, not-Son,
not-image, but as He is – sheer, pure, absolute
Oneness, without any duality. ”

MEISTER ECKHART

" For those who look with their physical eyes,
God is nowhere to be seen.
For those who contemplate Him in spirit,
He is everywhere.
He is in all, yet beyond all. "

ST. SYMEON

*Only wonder can comprehend
His incomprehensible power.*

MAXIMUS THE CONFESSOR

" What does God do all day long?
He gives birth.
From the beginning of eternity
God lies on a maternity bed
giving birth to the All.

God is creating this whole universe,
full and entire,
in this present moment. "

MEISTER ECKHART

*If your heart is straight with God, then
every creature will appear to you as a
mirror of life and a sacred scripture.
No creature is so small and insignificant
so as not to express and demonstrate the
goodness of God.*

THOMAS À KEMPIS

*It is greater worship to God to see Him in
all things, than in any special thing.*

MOTHER JULIAN OF NORWICH

*I am that which is highest.
I am that which is lowest.
I am that which is All.*

GOD SPEAKING TO MOTHER
JULIAN OF NORWICH

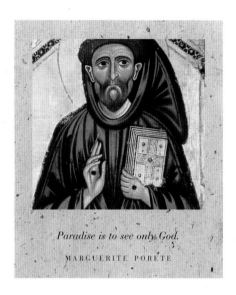

Paradise is to see only God.

MARGUERITE PORETE

❝ I have seen the One who is, and how He is the being
of all creatures. God is present in everything that exists, in a
devil and a good angel, in heaven and hell, in good deeds
and in adultery and murder, in the beautiful and the ugly.
Therefore, while I am in this Truth, I take as much delight
in seeing and understanding his presence in a devil and the
act of adultery as I do in an angel and a good deed. ❞

ANGELA OF FOLIGNO

15

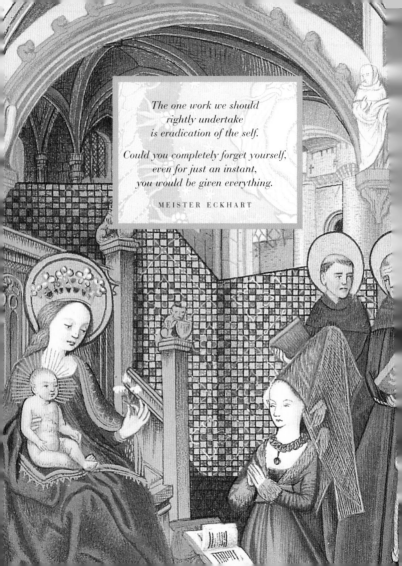

The one work we should
rightly undertake
is eradication of the self.

Could you completely forget yourself,
even for just an instant,
you would be given everything.

MEISTER ECKHART

The Protestant cobbler Jacob Boehme
experienced a spiritual awakening when he saw
sunlight reflecting on the water of a pewter dish
and perceived God as the unmanifest unity
which reflects itself in its creation. Previous to
creation, Boehme taught, God was without
knowledge of Himself. Creation is God coming to
consciousness of Himself, that fully occurs when
a human being completely awakens in an
experience of ecstatic love.

The world is pregnant with God.

ANGELA OF FOLIGNO

II Communion

The goal of mysticism is communion with God. In this experience, the mystic no longer exists as a separate individual, but becomes one with the Oneness. This vision can only arise when the mystic realises that the ego–self is only an illusionary veil that masks the true divine Self; and that this Self is God, the Being of all beings. God is not something "other," but is our shared essential identity. Communion with God is experienced as freedom from suffering the separation of solitary confinement within the mortal self, and blissful liberation into the expansive, all–embracing, eternal nature of God.

> *The human being is an animal who has received the vocation to become God.*
>
> BASIL OF CAESAREA

> The liberated soul loses her name in the One
> through Whom and in Whom she merges:
> just as a river reaching the sea
> loses the identity with which it flowed
> through many countries
> to arrive at this destination.
> Now it is in the sea,
> and here it rests without labor.

MARGUERITE PORETE

66 Just as someone who looks at the sun cannot
avoid filling his eyes with light, so someone
who always intently contemplates his own heart
cannot fail to be illuminated. 99

ST. HESYCHIOS THE PRIEST

66 God inhabits every soul, even those of the greatest
sinners is the world. There is always this union between
God and His creatures, for through it He preserves
their being. If it were not so, these souls would
instantly cease to be. 99

ST. JOHN OF THE CROSS

*The passing life of the senses doesn't lead
to knowledge of what our Self is. When we
clearly see what our Self is, then we shall
truly know our Lord God in great joy.*

MOTHER JULIAN OF NORWICH

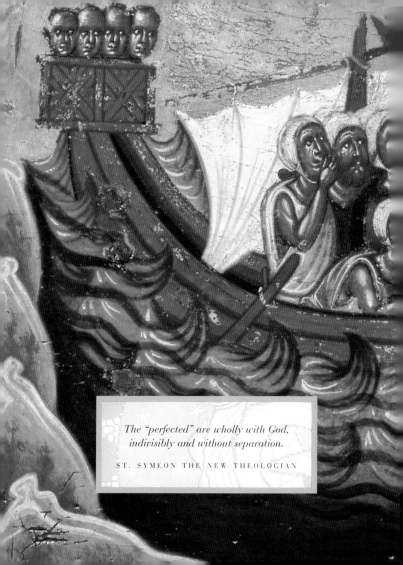

The "perfected" are wholly with God,
indivisibly and without separation.

ST. SYMEON THE NEW THEOLOGIAN

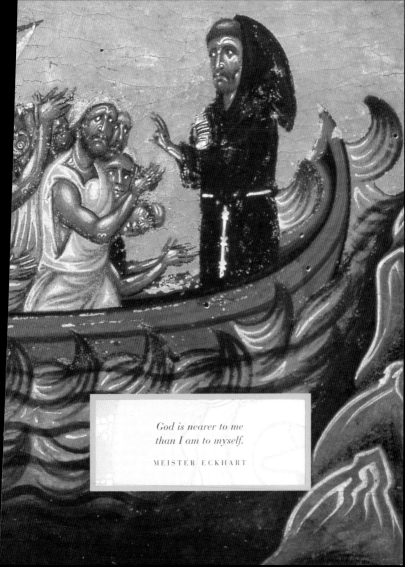

God is nearer to me
than I am to myself.

MEISTER ECKHART

66 Our essential nature is uncreated, never-born, and
free in and for itself. It is found in all creatures,
but is not restricted to them; it is outside all
creatures, but not excluded from them. 99

THE CLOUD OF UNKNOWING

66 The ineffable sweetness of perfect union cannot
be described with the tongue, which is a finite thing.
Lovely beyond loveliness is the home of the soul in perfect
union with Me. Nothing stands between us,
because she has become one thing with Me. 99

GOD SPEAKING TO CATHERINE OF SIENNA

My soul then said, "I have nothing,
for I am utterly stripped and naked;
I can do nothing for I have no manner
of power, but am as water poured out;
I am nothing, for all that I am is no
more than an image of Being,
and only God is my I AM."

JACOB BOEHME

Simple people imagine that they should see
God as if He stood there and they here.
This is not so. God and I, we are one.

MEISTER ECKHART

When the soul has lost her nature in
the Oneness, we can no longer speak of
a "soul," but of immeasurable Being.

MEISTER ECKHART

I AM can be spoken by no creature,
but by God alone. I must become God and
God must become me, so completely that
we share the same "I" eternally.
Our truest "I" is God.

MEISTER ECKHART

66 The more you abandon yourself,
the more you will find Me.
You are that which is not.
I am that I am. 99

GOD SPEAKING
TO CATHERINE OF SIENNA

Someone who is joined to the Lord
is One Spirit.

ST. PAUL

I discovered myself to be
nothing but nothing;
an unweighable substance;
a sea that cannot be sailed.
In You and by You,
I find that I exist as
nothing but nothing.

THOMAS À KEMPIS

Only total death to self leads to being
completely lost in God.

MADAME GUYON

I am as rich as God
for there is no grain of dust
that I do not share
in common with him.

ANGELUS SILESIUS

III The Mystic Path

For the mystics, religion is not just a matter of creeds and rituals, it is a spiritual path to experiential knowledge of God. It is the process of eradicating all the selfishness that binds us to our illusionary separate identities and blinds us to the omnipresent Oneness. To walk this way we must abandon our own personal desires and completely accept all that God wills. More than this, we must realize that self-will is ultimately an illusion, for as the 14th-century mystic Mother Julian of Norwich says "Our Lord God does everything."

> ❝ What good is it to me if Mary gave birth to the Son of God hundreds of years ago, if I do not give birth to the Son of God in my time and my culture.
>
> We are all meant to be Mothers of of God, for God is always needing to be born. ❞
>
> MEISTER ECKHART

St Francis of Assisi gave all to God and once appeared in church stark naked, referring to himself as "The Lord's Fool." He taught, "We are the mother of Christ when we carry him in our hearts with love and sincerity. We give birth to him through our good works, that should shine on others as an example."

66 Having read many books containing different
methods of reaching God, I felt that they would
confuse me rather than help me find what I was
looking for, which was to become completely
God's. This led me to resolve to give all for the All.
I renounced, for love of Him, everything that was
not Him, and I began to live as if there was
nothing but He and I in the world. 99

BROTHER LAWRENCE

Reprove yourself if ever the devil,
or your own shortsightedness, should
do you the disservice of making you
want to force all my servants to walk
by the same path as you yourself
follow, for this would be contrary to
the teachings given you by my Truth.

GOD SPEAKING
TO CATHERINE OF SIENNA

Someone who seeks for anything in
religion, other than God and the salvation
of his soul, will find nothing there but
sorrow and trouble.

THOMAS À KEMPIS

Do not draw consolation only from the
scriptures written in ink, for God's
grace also writes the laws of the Spirit
directly on the tablet of the heart.

PSEUDO-MACARIUS

*People should think less about what
they ought to do and more about what
they ought to be.*

MEISTER ECKHART

*You will never be satisfied
with impermanent, passing things,
for you were not created
to find your rest in them.*

THOMAS À KEMPIS

*What I know of the Divine
I learnt in the woods and fields.
I have no other masters
other than the beeches and the oaks.*

ST. BERNARD

66 Those overtaken by a storm when traveling
by sea don't worry about their luggage, but throw
it overboard with their own hands, considering
their property to be less important than their lives.
So why don't we, following this example, throw
out whatever drags our soul down to the depths. 99

ST. NELIOS THE ASCETIC

In the beginning of the spiritual life
we should faithfully do our duty
and deny ourselves, but after that
comes unspeakable pleasures.

BROTHER LAWRENCE

66 We must become truly poor and as free from our
own will as when we were born. I tell you,
by the eternal truth, so long as you even desire to
fulfil the will of God and hanker after eternity, you
are not truly poor. Only someone who wills
nothing, knows nothing, and desires nothing,
has true spiritual poverty. 99

MEISTER ECKHART

❝ As the light grows, we see ourselves to be worse than we thought. We are amazed at our former blindness as we see issuing from our heart a whole swarm of shameful feelings, like filthy reptiles crawling from a hidden cave. But we must be neither amazed nor disturbed. We are not worse than we were; on the contrary we are better. But while our faults diminish, the light we see them by waxes brighter, and we are filled with horror. **❞**

FÉNELON

If the only prayer you say in your whole life is "thank you," that would be enough.

MEISTER ECKHART

❝ Someone who will endure only so much as he pleases, and from whom he pleases, is not truly patient. A truly patient person accepts everything. He is not concerned if the person who afflicts him is a saint or a sinner. But whenever adversity comes his way, regardless of what it is, who it comes from, and how frequently, the truly patient person accepts everything as coming from the hand of God. **❞**

THOMAS À KEMPIS

To take pleasure in everything,
desire pleasure in nothing.

To possess everything,
desire to possess nothing.

To be everything,
desire to be nothing.

To know everything,
desire to know nothing.

ST. JOHN OF THE CROSS

“ We must not wish anything other than
what happens from moment to moment. ”

ST. CATHERINE OF GENOA

“ Humans see some deeds as good and others as evil,
but our Lord doesn't see things like this; for everything
is given its nature by God and so all that is done is done by
God. It is easy to understand that the best of deeds is well
done, but the least of deeds is as well done as the best,
for all thing happen in the way and order that our Lord has
ordained for them from beginningless time;
for there is no doer but Him. ”

MOTHER JULIAN OF NORWICH

*The liberated soul has
nothing to sin with,
for without a will no one can sin.*

MARGUERITE PORETE

*When Brother Lawrence failed in his
duty, he would only confess his fault by
saying to God "If you leave me to
myself, I cannot help but fall. It is You
that must hinder my falling and put
right what is amiss." After this he gave
himself no further uneasiness about it.*

*I will only your wellbeing and whatever
I give to you I give it so that you may
reach the goal for which I created you.*

GOD SPEAKING TO
CATHERINE OF SIENNA

· S ·

BONAVEN
TVRA

*The tall tower of virtue cannot
stand long unless it is based on the
low foundation of humility.*

THOMAS À KEMPIS

IV Humility

Humility is a central Christian virtue because it decreases the power of the separate self and so unites us with God. Humility is not about putting ourselves down, but about lifting ourselves up. It is not neurotic self-depreciation, but simply seeing our ego-self for what it is – a small part of the greater whole. When we serve and take pride in our self, we are bound to the illusion of separateness that divides us from our true nature. When we humbly reduce ourselves to nothing, we expand to experience ourselves as everything though communion with God.

> *Choose the meekness of Moses*
> *and you will discover your heart of rock*
> *is transformed into a spring of water.*
>
> AMMA SYNCLETICA

*I have seen uneducated people who
were truly humble and they became
the wisest of the wise. I have also seen
other uneducated persons, hearing this
praise, pride themselves on their lack
of education and fall into arrogance.*

ST. MARK THE ASCETIC

*Humble self-knowledge is a surer way to
God than searching the depths of learning.*

THOMAS À KEMPIS

*No harm comes from holding yourself
to be less than someone else,
even if it is not true; but much harm
comes from holding yourself to be
better than others, even if they
are great sinners.*

THOMAS À KEMPIS

      "A hermit who could cast out demons asked them,
"Is it fasting that gives me the power to banish you?"
The demons replied, "We do not eat."
He asked, "Is it vigils?"
The demons replied, "We do not sleep."
He asked, "Is it retreat from the world?"
The demons replied, "We live in the deserts."
He asked, "What is it, then, that gives me power over you?"
The demons replied, "Nothing can overcome us
but humility."

AMMA THEODORA

41

“ The liberated see gold and ignore its gleaming,
understanding that it is stuff of the earth,
no more than dust and clay.
Seeing someone puffed up with pride
being carried on a throne in solemn procession,
they regard it all as a dream.
They smile and are astonished
at the ignorance of humanity. ”

ST. SYMEON THE NEW THEOLOGIAN

66 Humility unites humanity with God.
Like St. John the Baptist, we should say,
"We must decrease, so He may increase." 99

ST. DIADOCHOS OF PHOTIKI

66 If only we could understand how
our self-righteousness is the very opposite
of God's purpose. 99

MADAME GUYON

*He doesn't want us to busy ourselves with
self-accusation about our sins, and feeling
wretched about ourselves, but to quickly
turn ourselves to Him.*

MOTHER JULIAN OF NORWICH

66 Remember this and you will never judge another:
Judas was once an apostle and the thief crucified at
Christ's side was once a murderer. 99

JOHN CLIMACUS

v Mystical Prayer

For the mystics, prayer is more than petitioning an all-powerful deity with their personal desires. It is a technique to come into communion with the Being of all beings. God is no-thing and so is beyond any particular image that the mind can create. Thoughts and images cannot reveal God, but rather conceal His naked presence. God is not understood with the intellect, but intuitively known when thoughts are absent. Mystical prayer is emptying the mind so that we may directly experience Consciousness itself; the nothingness that contains everything.

> *Every concept grasped by the mind*
> *becomes an obstacle in the quest*
> *to those who search.*
>
> GREGORY OF NYSSA

> **"** If even only for a moment you can throw yourself into
> That in which there are no separate beings, then you will
> hear what God says. Just stop all your thinking and willing,
> and you will hear the unspeakable words of God. **"**

JACOB BOEHME

> **"** If you try to understand the naked being of the soul
> empty of all self, it will fly away from you; but if you
> completely surrender to it, then it will stay with you
> and naturally become the Life of your life. **"**

JACOB BOEHME

> *When St. John says that God is a spirit and must be worshiped in spirit, he means that the mind must be cleared of all images. When you pray, shut the door of the senses against all fantasies and thoughts. Nothing pleases God more than a mind free from distractions. Such a mind is transformed into God, because it can think of nothing, understand nothing, love nothing, except God; seeing other creatures and itself only in God.*

ALBERTUS MAGNUS

To come into union with the wisdom
of God, the soul has to embrace
not-knowing, rather than knowledge.

ST. JOHN OF THE CROSS

When is someone in mere
understanding?
When things are seen as separate
one from the other.
When is someone above mere
understanding?
When all is seen in All.

MEISTER ECKHART

Hold your self in prayer before God,
like a dumb or paralytic beggar
at a rich man's gate.

BROTHER LAWRENCE

It is better for the soul
to be in the sweet country
of understanding nothing.

MARGUERITE PORETE

66 The blessed divine light will illuminate the heart
to the degree that pure Consciousness is purged of all
concepts and ideas. 99

ST. HESYCHIOS THE PRIEST

66 Be still and know.
Remain in a state of spiritual wakefulness,
with your mind and senses open,
to hear what God wills in every moment. 99

ABBOT VASILIOS

 49

VI Love

At the heart of Christian mysticism is the power of love. Love embraces everything without reservation. Love propels us beyond our limited self-interest and unites us with others. To experience love is to die to oneself and to live in God. When love fills the heart our lives are naturally God-inspired, and we can do no wrong, for God is love. The mystics delight in a divine love affair with God, who is their affectionate spouse and constant friend. They fall in love with Love, and in this loving all separation is transcended. Lover and beloved dissolve into each other and only Love remains.

Blessed is the person whose desire
for God has become like the
lover's passion for the beloved.

JOHN CLIMACUS

My mercy is incomparably greater than
all the sins you could commit.

GOD SPEAKING TO
CATHERINE OF SIENNA

66 Fasting, vigils, the study of scripture, renouncing
possessions and the world – these are the means not the end.
Perfection is not found in them, but through them.
It is pointless to boast about such practices when we have
not achieved the love of God and our fellow humans.
Those who have achieved love of God within themselves,
are always mindful of God. 99

ST. JOHN CASSIAN

If Love kindles a fire in you,
you will feel it burning up your self
and devouring all ego –
all of that which you call "I" and "me."

JACOB BOEHME

66 God cannot be comprehended by the faculty
of intelligence, but is totally and perfectly intelligible
through the power of love. Every single creature, moreover
will know him differently. Dwell on this if you have the grace
to do so, because to experience this for oneself is everlasting
joy, and the contrary is everlasting pain. 99

THE CLOUD OF UNKNOWING

Love is infallible.
It commits no errors,
for all errors
are want of love.

WILLIAM LAW

66 The plan of divine love is to draw back to itself
that which it loves: it draws everyone out of themselves and
out of all created reality, and totally into the uncreated. 99

ANGELA OF FOLIGNO

53

God is love
and those that live in love
live in God
and God lives in them.

ST. JOHN

The mystery of God hugs you
in its all-encompassing arms.

HILDEGARD DE BINGEN

God loves us infinitely more
than we can possibly imagine.

BROTHER LAWRENCE

When you reach perfection I will relieve
you of this lover's game of togetherness
and separation.

GOD SPEAKING TO

CATHERINE OF SIENNA

  66 Those who consciously love God in their hearts
never lose an intense longing for spiritual illumination,
until they feel it in their bones and no longer know
themselves but are completely transformed by the love of
God. They are both present in this life and not present.
They live in the body, but have departed from it, as through
love they ceaselessly journey in their souls towards God.
Their hearts constantly burn with the fire of love and
they cling to God with an irresistible fervor, for they have,
once and for all, transcended self-love
in their love for God. **99**

ST. DIADOCHOS OF PHOTIKI

“ It is one thing not to be angered by insults,
it is another to be pleased by them.
It is one thing to pray for people who act badly,
and another to completely love them as benefactors;
and still another to impress on one's soul their faces, and
with tears of real love to embrace them as true friends. ”

ST. SYMEON THE NEW THEOLOGIAN

*Do you know how to tell if your spiritual
love is not perfect? Observe if you are
distressed when you see that those you love
are not returning your love or not loving
you as much as you think you love them; or
when you feel you are being deprived of
their company and comfort, or that they
love another more than you.*

CATHERINE OF SIENNA

“ Our only business is to love
and delight ourselves in God. ”

BROTHER LAWRENCE

Between Almighty God and a devoted soul
pass many spiritual visits,
sweet inward conversations,
great gifts of grace,
many consolations,
much heavenly peace,
and wonderful intimacy
with the blessed presence.

THOMAS À KEMPIS

“ You cannot possibly have any ill-temper, or show any
unkind behaviour to a man for whose welfare you are so
much concerned, as to be his advocate with God in private.
For you cannot possibly despise and ridicule that man
whom your private prayers recommend to
the love and favor of God. ”

WILLIAM LAW

“ My soul then heard these words: "My beautiful spouse,
who I love so affectionately,
don't come to me carrying sorrow and suffering,
but rejoicing in ineffable joy."
He then showed me the robe
that the bridegroom shows to the bride;
it was not of purple or scarlet,
but of marvelous light to cloth my soul.
"It is right for a king to wed his long-loved bride
clothed in royal garments," He said. ”

ANGELA OF FOLIGNO

I am your playmate.
I will lead the child within you
on a wonderful adventure
that I have chosen for you.

GOD SPEAKING TO

MECHTILD OF MAGDEBURG

My Beloved is the high mountains.
and the lonely valley forests:
unexplored islands, rushing rivers,
and the love songs of the wind:
the hushed night-time
and the waking dawn:
the soundless music of silent solitude:
the supper that nourishes
and swells me with love.

ST. JOHN OF THE CROSS

Love and do what you will.

ST. AUGUSTINE

The publishers would like to thank the following for the use of pictures:

e.t. archive: pp. 5, 11, 13, 15, 22, 29, 30, 35, 36, 38, 41, 42, 46, 49,
51, 53, 57, 58, 59, 60
Vanessa Fletcher: pp. 4, 10, 16, 17, 19, 20, 21, 24, 55